T0327283

FERNHURST

BOOKS

LOGBOOK

for GPS Navigation

Compact, for Small Chart Tables

Devised by Bill Anderson

Log of the Yacht

COMPILING THE LOG

This logbook consists of pairs of pages: the left-hand page is for passage planning and the right-hand page is for navigational records. Planning and execution have been combined in this way so that for the most common pattern of cruising, with passages which can be completed within 24 hours, you have everything on a single opening for easy reference. On longer passages the left-hand page can be used for additional narrative.

At the end of the book is a section for notes on pilotage, harbours, anchorages and other details. There is also a visitors' book.

Pages 4 and 5 give an example of how the passage planning and navigational records pages might be used.

PASSAGE PLANNING CHECKLIST (left-hand pages)

Every passage is different and you will not need to consider every item in the checklist for every passage. The order in which you do the planning will also vary. On one passage the crucial factor will be the height of tide, on another it will be the time of tidal stream change through a race and on a third it will be the hours of daylight and darkness for harbour departure or entry. In many cases the main decisions such as time to set out and route to take will be made for totally non-navigational reasons such as the time at which crew members prefer to get out of their bunks in the morning or the sightseeing opportunities along the coast.

1. General outline
- Departure point and destination. Possible diversions for shelter or repairs.
- Overall distance. Likely time to complete (approx.).
- For long voyages, is insurance valid for destination, do all crew have necessary visas?

2. Charts and publications
- Check that GPS is set to same datum as charts. Note any different datums used for plans in sailing directions and other navigational publications.
- Charts required.
  (Check corrections up to date.)
- Sailing directions required.
  (Check corrections up to date.)
- Other navigational publications.
  (Check that they are latest available.)

The charts and sailing directions will identify the probable detailed route and will indicate areas where tidal factors need careful consideration. Mark the pages in the sailing directions for reference on passage. (A piece of masking tape is ideal - it doesn't blow away and at the end of the passage it can be removed without damaging the book.)

3. Tidal considerations
Tidal heights
- Times of high and low water for departure point, destination and any possible diversion ports.
- Times between which ports or their approaches are unavailable due to insufficient rise of tide.
- Times between which bridges or overhead obstructions are a hazard due to excessive rise of tide.

Tidal streams
- Times at which streams are favourable.
- Times at which areas of fast tidal stream are impassable.
- Times at which rate and direction of flow may create hazards (e.g. ebb stream over river bar, particularly with onshore wind or swell).

4. Weather
- Weather forecast. (Update whenever possible.)
- Is the passage sensible with the current forecast?

5. The detailed route
- Navigational hazards. Examine the charts in detail, highlight any hazards close to the likely track and plan how to clear them safely.
- Select Waypoints to define the route and enter in GPS.
- Combine the Waypoints into a Route and note the number in the GPS for future retrieval.
- Check bearing and distance of each leg given by GPS against bearing and distance on the chart (to guard against errors in reading off positions or entering them in the GPS).
- Times of daylight and darkness.
- Moonlight (time of rising and setting and phase).
- Are any areas impassable or particularly hazardous in darkness?
- Decide departure time and estimated time of arrival.
- Note any critical times for passing through tidal gates.

- If you can make a reasonable prediction of speed, work out course to steer for cross-tide legs.

NAVIGATIONAL RECORDS
(right-hand pages)

The purpose of these pages is to keep a navigational record in sufficient detail for you to pick up the navigation by conventional means if the GPS fails. You will also be able to reconstruct the track followed by the yacht if you ever need to show where she was at any particular time. In addition, the pages contain columns to record basic Met. information which will help in interpreting forecasts and monitoring the progress of nearby weather systems.

PILOTAGE, HARBOUR, ANCHORAGE AND OTHER NOTES (pages 84 - 89)

Different navigators will want to use these lightly-ruled pages in different ways. Some may keep a record (with sketch plans, drawings or photographs) of harbours and anchorages for which no large-scale charts exist. Others may simply want to make a note of the phone numbers of their favourite restaurants for future bookings. In any event, there is always a need to keep notes which do not fit into any convenient category.

THE VISITORS' BOOK
(pages 90 – 95)

If you are using this section as a visitors' book no explanation is needed. If you make frequent crew changes you may also wish to use it as a record of those joining and leaving.

PASSAGE PLAN FROM *Weymouth* TO *Newtown River, IoW* DATE *2nd June*

	ROUTE:	CRSE(M)	DIST	CHECKED
Distance approx 42' = 7hrs at 6kn	WEYMOUTH			
Critical factors: tidal stream at St Albans Hd, Anvil Pt and Hurst		103°	15'	YES
Possible diversions: Poole, Yarmouth IoW or Lymington	ST ALBANS			
CHARTS: 5601.4, 5601.5, 5600.4, 5600.5.		089°	4.1'	YES
SAILING DIRECTIONS: Shell Channel Pilot	ANVIL PT			
TIDAL STREAMS: Ref port Dover, HW 0443 & 1706, Range		074°	13'	YES
3.6m (neaps). Stream turns fair at St Albans at 1030, foul at	NEEDLES			
Newtown at 1600. Tidal streams weak in Weymouth Bay.		051°	4.2'	YES
TIDAL HEIGHTS (not critical)	HURST			
Weymouth 0501 0.6m 1154 1.3m		070°	1.3'	YES
Poole LWs 1004 1.0m 2137 1.2m	YARMOUTH			
Portsmouth 1019 1.6m 1725 4.0m		072°	3.0'	YES
Corrections -18 -0.3m -09 -1.1m	HAMSTEAD			
Newtown 1001 1.3m 1716 2.9m		124°	0.9'	YES
WAYPOINTS:	NEWTOWN			
WEYENT 50° 36'.6 N 02° 26'.4 W	**WAYPOINTS** for diversion or change of route:			
STALB 50° 34'.4 N 02° 03'.3 W	POOLE 50° 39'.0 N 01° 54'.5 W			
ANVPT 50° 34'.8 N 01° 56'.9W	NORCHA 50° 42'.6 N 01° 35'.4 W			
NEEDLE 50° 39'.4 N 01° 37'.1 W	**TIMINGS:** Pass St Albans 1030, therefore depart Weymouth 0700			
HURST 50° 42'.25 N 01° 32'.3 W	Pass Needles 1330, Hurst 1415, arrive Newtown 1515.			
YARM 50° 42'.8 N 01° 30'.4 W	**WEATHER FORECAST.** Issued at 011730, SW 4-5, Fair, Good.			
HAMLED 50° 43'.95 N 01° 26'.0 W	If wind >F6 enter Solent through North Channel, not Needles.			
NEWTN 50° 43'.5 N 01° 24'.75W				

TIME	CRSE T/M/C	LOG DIST	LAT/LONG OR WPT BRG/DST	NARRATIVE	WIND	BAR
0700	-	-	-	On engine. Slipped. Motored out of Weymouth		
0725	105°	0	-	Off Engine, set full main and genoa	SW4	1017
0800	105°	2.5	STALB 102° 12.5'			
0900	105°	8.1	STALB 100° 7.4'	A/C 100°(M)	SW4	1017
1000	100°	14.0	STALB 099° 2.3'			
1023	100°	15.9	At STALB WP	A/C 090°		
1105	090°	19.5	At ANVL WP	A/C 075° Wind increasing	SW5	1016
1200	075°	25.3	NEEDLE 073° 7.1'	Visual fix agrees with Wpt bearing and distance.		
1300	075°	31.4	At NEEDLE WP	A/C 050° into Needles Channel	SW5	1016
1335	050°	34.6	At HURST WP	A/C 070° into Solent		
1420	070°	39.1		Approaching Hamstead Ledge. On engine. Stowed sails.		
				Motored into Newtown River		
1500				Secured to visitors' buoy. Off engine.		

Engine Hours c/f 14.3 **Today** 1.1 **Total** 15.4

PASSAGE PLAN FROM .... **TO** .... **DATE** ....

FROM.................. **TOWARDS**.................. **DATE**.......... **ZONE**...... **DATUM**......... **VAR**.......

TIME	CRSE T/M/C	LOG DIST	LAT/LONG OR WPT BRG/DST	NARRATIVE	WIND	BAR

Engine Hours c/f............ Today............ Total.............

PASSAGE PLAN FROM .... **TO** .... **DATE** ....

FROM................. **TOWARDS**.................. **DATE** .... **ZONE**...... **DATUM**......... **VAR**.......

TIME	CRSE T/M/C	LOG DIST	LAT/LONG OR WPT BRG/DST	NARRATIVE	WIND	BAR

Engine Hours c/f............ Today............ Total............

PASSAGE PLAN FROM .... **TO** .... **DATE** ....

FROM.................. **TOWARDS**.................. **DATE** .... **ZONE**...... **DATUM**......... **VAR**.......

TIME	CRSE T/M/C	LOG DIST	LAT/LONG OR WPT BRG/DST	NARRATIVE	WIND	BAR

Engine Hours c/f............ Today............ Total.............

PASSAGE PLAN FROM .... **TO** .... **DATE** ....

FROM.................. **TOWARDS**.................. **DATE**.......... **ZONE**....... **DATUM**.......... **VAR**........

TIME	CRSE T/M/C	LOG DIST	LAT/LONG OR WPT BRG/DST	NARRATIVE	WIND	BAR

Engine Hours c/f............. Today............ Total..............

PASSAGE PLAN FROM .... **TO** .... **DATE** ....

FROM.................. **TOWARDS**.................. **DATE**......... **ZONE**...... **DATUM**......... **VAR**.......

TIME	CRSE T/M/C	LOG DIST	LAT/LONG OR WPT BRG/DST	NARRATIVE	WIND	BAR

Engine Hours c/f............ Today............ Total..............

PASSAGE PLAN FROM .... **TO** .... **DATE** ....

FROM.................. **TOWARDS**.................. **DATE** .... **ZONE**...... **DATUM**.......... **VAR**........

TIME	CRSE T/M/C	LOG DIST	LAT/LONG OR WPT BRG/DST	NARRATIVE	WIND	BAR

Engine Hours c/f............ **Today**............ **Total**.............

17

PASSAGE PLAN FROM .... **TO** .... **DATE** ....

FROM.................... TOWARDS.................... DATE .... ZONE...... DATUM.......... VAR........

TIME	CRSE T/M/C	LOG DIST	LAT/LONG OR WPT BRG/DST	NARRATIVE	WIND	BAR

Engine Hours c/f............ Today............ Total............

PASSAGE PLAN FROM .... **TO** .... **DATE** ....

FROM.................. **TOWARDS**.................. **DATE** .... **ZONE**...... **DATUM**.......... **VAR**.......

TIME	CRSE T/M/C	LOG DIST	LAT/LONG OR WPT BRG/DST	NARRATIVE	WIND	BAR

Engine Hours c/f............ **Today**............ **Total**.............

PASSAGE PLAN FROM .... **TO** .... **DATE** ....

FROM.................. **TOWARDS**.................. **DATE** .... **ZONE**...... **DATUM**.......... **VAR**.......

TIME	CRSE T/M/C	LOG DIST	LAT/LONG OR WPT BRG/DST	NARRATIVE	WIND	BAR

Engine Hours c/f............ **Today**............ **Total**.............

PASSAGE PLAN FROM .... TO .... DATE ....

FROM.................. **TOWARDS**.................. **DATE** .... **ZONE** ...... **DATUM** .... **VAR** ....

TIME	CRSE T/M/C	LOG DIST	LAT/LONG OR WPT BRG/DST	NARRATIVE	WIND	BAR

Engine Hours c/f............ **Today**............ **Total**............

PASSAGE PLAN FROM .... **TO** .... **DATE** ....

FROM.................. TOWARDS.................. DATE .... ZONE...... DATUM......... VAR.......

TIME	CRSE T/M/C	LOG DIST	LAT/LONG OR WPT BRG/DST	NARRATIVE	WIND	BAR

Engine Hours c/f............ Today............ Total.............

PASSAGE PLAN FROM .... **TO** .... **DATE** ....

FROM.................. TOWARDS................... DATE .... ZONE....... DATUM.......... VAR........

TIME	CRSE T/M/C	LOG DIST	LAT/LONG OR WPT BRG/DST	NARRATIVE	WIND	BAR

Engine Hours c/f............ Today............ Total.............

PASSAGE PLAN FROM .... **TO** .... **DATE** ....

FROM.................. TOWARDS................... DATE .... ZONE...... DATUM......... VAR.......

TIME	CRSE T/M/C	LOG DIST	LAT/LONG OR WPT BRG/DST	NARRATIVE	WIND	BAR

Engine Hours c/f............ Today............ Total.............

PASSAGE PLAN FROM .... **TO** .... **DATE** ....

FROM................. **TOWARDS**.................. **DATE** .... **ZONE**...... **DATUM**......... **VAR**.......

TIME	CRSE T/M/C	LOG DIST	LAT/LONG OR WPT BRG/DST	NARRATIVE	WIND	BAR

Engine Hours c/f............ Today............ Total.............

PASSAGE PLAN FROM .... TO .... DATE ....

FROM.................. **TOWARDS**.................. **DATE** .... **ZONE**...... **DATUM**......... **VAR**.......

TIME	CRSE T/M/C	LOG DIST	LAT/LONG OR WPT BRG/DST	NARRATIVE	WIND	BAR

Engine Hours c/f............ Today............ Total.............

PASSAGE PLAN FROM .... **TO** .... **DATE** ....

FROM.................. **TOWARDS**.................. **DATE** .... **ZONE**...... **DATUM**......... **VAR**.......

TIME	CRSE T/M/C	LOG DIST	LAT/LONG OR WPT BRG/DST	NARRATIVE	WIND	BAR

Engine Hours c/f............ **Today**............ **Total**.............

PASSAGE PLAN FROM .... **TO** .... **DATE** ....

FROM.................. **TOWARDS**.................. **DATE** .... **ZONE**...... **DATUM**......... **VAR**.......

TIME	CRSE T/M/C	LOG DIST	LAT/LONG OR WPT BRG/DST	NARRATIVE	WIND	BAR

Engine Hours c/f............ Today............ Total.............

39

PASSAGE PLAN FROM .... **TO** .... **DATE** ....

FROM.................. **TOWARDS**.................. **DATE**.......... **ZONE**....... **DATUM**.......... **VAR**........

TIME	CRSE T/M/C	LOG DIST	LAT/LONG OR WPT BRG/DST	NARRATIVE	WIND	BAR

Engine Hours c/f............. Today............ Total.............

PASSAGE PLAN FROM .... **TO** .... **DATE** ....

FROM................. **TOWARDS**................... **DATE**.......... **ZONE**...... **DATUM**.......... **VAR**........

TIME	CRSE T/M/C	LOG DIST	LAT/LONG OR WPT BRG/DST	NARRATIVE	WIND	BAR

Engine Hours c/f............ **Today**............ **Total**.............

PASSAGE PLAN FROM .... **TO** .... **DATE** ....

FROM.................. **TOWARDS**.................. **DATE**.......... **ZONE**....... **DATUM**.......... **VAR**.......

TIME	CRSE T/M/C	LOG DIST	LAT/LONG OR WPT BRG/DST	NARRATIVE	WIND	BAR

Engine Hours c/f............ Today............ Total.............

PASSAGE PLAN FROM .... **TO** .... **DATE** ....

FROM.................. **TOWARDS**.................. **DATE** .... **ZONE**...... **DATUM**......... **VAR**........

TIME	CRSE T/M/C	LOG DIST	LAT/LONG OR WPT BRG/DST	NARRATIVE	WIND	BAR

Engine Hours c/f............ **Today**............ **Total**..............

PASSAGE PLAN FROM .... **TO** .... **DATE** ....

FROM.................. **TOWARDS**.................. **DATE** .... **ZONE**...... **DATUM**.......... **VAR**.......

TIME	CRSE T/M/C	LOG DIST	LAT/LONG OR WPT BRG/DST	NARRATIVE	WIND	BAR

Engine Hours c/f............ **Today**............ **Total**...........

PASSAGE PLAN FROM .... **TO** .... **DATE** ....

FROM.................. **TOWARDS**.................. **DATE** .... **ZONE**...... **DATUM**.......... **VAR**........

TIME	CRSE T/M/C	LOG DIST	LAT/LONG OR WPT BRG/DST	NARRATIVE	WIND	BAR

Engine Hours c/f............ **Today**............ **Total**............

PASSAGE PLAN FROM .... TO .... DATE ....

FROM.................. TOWARDS.................. DATE .... ZONE...... DATUM.......... VAR.......

TIME	CRSE T/M/C	LOG DIST	LAT/LONG OR WPT BRG/DST	NARRATIVE	WIND	BAR

Engine Hours c/f............ Today............ Total............

PASSAGE PLAN FROM .... **TO** .... **DATE** ....

FROM.................. TOWARDS.................. DATE .... ZONE...... DATUM.......... VAR.......

TIME	CRSE T/M/C	LOG DIST	LAT/LONG OR WPT BRG/DST	NARRATIVE	WIND	BAR

Engine Hours c/f............ Today............ Total.............

PASSAGE PLAN FROM .... **TO** .... **DATE** ....

FROM.................. TOWARDS.................. DATE .... ZONE...... DATUM.......... VAR........

TIME	CRSE T/M/C	LOG DIST	LAT/LONG OR WPT BRG/DST	NARRATIVE	WIND	BAR

Engine Hours c/f............ Today............ Total............

PASSAGE PLAN FROM .... **TO** .... **DATE** ....

FROM.................. TOWARDS.................. DATE .... ZONE...... DATUM.......... VAR........

TIME	CRSE T/M/C	LOG DIST	LAT/LONG OR WPT BRG/DST	NARRATIVE	WIND	BAR

Engine Hours c/f............ Today............ Total.............

PASSAGE PLAN FROM .... **TO** .... **DATE** ....

FROM.................. TOWARDS.................. DATE .... ZONE...... DATUM.......... VAR........

TIME	CRSE T/M/C	LOG DIST	LAT/LONG OR WPT BRG/DST	NARRATIVE	WIND	BAR

Engine Hours c/f............ Today............ Total.............

PASSAGE PLAN FROM .... **TO** .... **DATE** ....

FROM.................. **TOWARDS**.................. **DATE** .... **ZONE**....... **DATUM**.......... **VAR**.......

TIME	CRSE T/M/C	LOG DIST	LAT/LONG OR WPT BRG/DST	NARRATIVE	WIND	BAR

Engine Hours c/f............ **Today**............ **Total**.............

PASSAGE PLAN FROM .... **TO** .... **DATE** ....

FROM.................. TOWARDS.................. DATE .... ZONE...... DATUM......... VAR........

TIME	CRSE T/M/C	LOG DIST	LAT/LONG OR WPT BRG/DST	NARRATIVE	WIND	BAR

Engine Hours c/f............ Today............ Total.............

PASSAGE PLAN FROM .... **TO** .... **DATE** ....

FROM.................. **TOWARDS**.................. **DATE** .... **ZONE**...... **DATUM**.......... **VAR**........

TIME	CRSE T/M/C	LOG DIST	LAT/LONG OR WPT BRG/DST	NARRATIVE	WIND	BAR

Engine Hours c/f............ Today............ Total.............

PASSAGE PLAN FROM .... TO .... DATE ....

FROM.................. **TOWARDS**.................. **DATE** .... **ZONE**...... **DATUM**.......... **VAR**.......

TIME	CRSE T/M/C	LOG DIST	LAT/LONG OR WPT BRG/DST	NARRATIVE	WIND	BAR

Engine Hours c/f............ **Today**............ **Total**.............

PASSAGE PLAN FROM .... **TO** .... **DATE** ....

FROM.................. **TOWARDS**.................. **DATE** .... **ZONE**...... **DATUM**.......... **VAR**........

TIME	CRSE T/M/C	LOG DIST	LAT/LONG OR WPT BRG/DST	NARRATIVE	WIND	BAR

Engine Hours c/f............ Today............ Total.............

PASSAGE PLAN FROM .... **TO** .... **DATE** ....

FROM.................. **TOWARDS**.................. **DATE** .... **ZONE**...... **DATUM**......... **VAR**.......

TIME	CRSE T/M/C	LOG DIST	LAT/LONG OR WPT BRG/DST	NARRATIVE	WIND	BAR

Engine Hours c/f............ **Today**............ **Total**.............

PASSAGE PLAN FROM .... **TO** .... **DATE** ....

FROM.................... **TOWARDS**.................... **DATE**.......... **ZONE**...... **DATUM**.......... **VAR**........

TIME	CRSE T/M/C	LOG DIST	LAT/LONG OR WPT BRG/DST	NARRATIVE	WIND	BAR

Engine Hours c/f............ **Today**............ **Total**............

FROM.................. **TOWARDS**.................. **DATE**.......... **ZONE**....... **DATUM**.......... **VAR**........

TIME	CRSE T/M/C	LOG DIST	LAT/LONG OR WPT BRG/DST	NARRATIVE	WIND	BAR

Engine Hours c/f............ **Today**............ **Total**.............

PASSAGE PLAN FROM .... **TO** .... **DATE** ....

FROM.................. **TOWARDS**.................. **DATE**.......... **ZONE**....... **DATUM**.......... **VAR**........

TIME	CRSE T/M/C	LOG DIST	LAT/LONG OR WPT BRG/DST	NARRATIVE	WIND	BAR

Engine Hours c/f............ **Today**............ **Total**............

PASSAGE PLAN FROM .... **TO** .... **DATE** ....

FROM.................. **TOWARDS**.................. **DATE** .... **ZONE** ...... **DATUM** .... **VAR** ....

TIME	CRSE T/M/C	LOG DIST	LAT/LONG OR WPT BRG/DST	NARRATIVE	WIND	BAR

Engine Hours c/f............ **Today**............ **Total**..............

PASSAGE PLAN FROM .... **TO** .... **DATE** ....

FROM.................. **TOWARDS**.................. **DATE** .... **ZONE**...... **DATUM**......... **VAR**.......

TIME	CRSE T/M/C	LOG DIST	LAT/LONG OR WPT BRG/DST	NARRATIVE	WIND	BAR

Engine Hours c/f............ **Today**............ **Total**............

PILOTAGE, HARBOUR, ANCHORAGE & OTHER NOTES

PILOTAGE, HARBOUR, ANCHORAGE & OTHER NOTES

PILOTAGE, HARBOUR, ANCHORAGE & OTHER NOTES

PILOTAGE, HARBOUR, ANCHORAGE & OTHER NOTES

VISITORS' BOOK

VISITORS' BOOK

VISITORS' BOOK

VISITORS' BOOK

VISITORS' BOOK

Reprinted in 2022 by Fernhurst Books Limited

Copyright © 2015 Fernhurst Books Limited

This second edition first published in 2015 by Fernhurst Books Limited
The Windmill, Mill Lane, Harbury, Leamington Spa, Warwickshire, CV33 9HP. UK.
Tel: +44 (0) 1926 337488 | www.fernhurstbooks.com

Previous edition first published in 2002 by Fernhurst Books, reprinted in 2011 by John Wiley & Sons Ltd

British Library Cataloguing in Publication Data
A catalogue record for this book is available from the British Library
ISBN 978-1-909911-18-5

Artwork by Intelligent Byte, Rachel Atkins & Daniel Stephen
Printed in Poland through JB Concept

ISBN 978-1-909911-18-5